LITTLE CULTURAL

ENVOYS' JOURNEY

ON THE SILK ROAD

# 丝路环游记

李国忠 著

四川大学出版社
SICHUAN UNIVERSITY PRESS

## 图书在版编目（CIP）数据

丝路环游记 / 李国忠著. — 成都：四川大学出版社，2024.1
ISBN 978-7-5690-6341-7

Ⅰ．①丝… Ⅱ．①李… Ⅲ．①英语课－中小学－教学参考资料 Ⅳ．① G634.413

中国国家版本馆 CIP 数据核字（2023）第 174826 号

书　　名：丝路环游记
　　　　　Silu Huanyou Ji
著　　者：李国忠
------------------------------------------------------------
选题策划：徐丹红　曹雪敏
责任编辑：曹雪敏
责任校对：于　俊
装帧设计：墨创文化
插图绘制：冯雨柔
责任印制：王　炜
------------------------------------------------------------
出版发行：四川大学出版社有限责任公司
　　　　　地址：成都市一环路南一段 24 号（610065）
　　　　　电话：（028）85408311（发行部）、85400276（总编室）
　　　　　电子邮箱：scupress@vip.163.com
　　　　　网址：https://press.scu.edu.cn
印前制作：四川胜翔数码印务设计有限公司
印刷装订：四川省平轩印务有限公司
------------------------------------------------------------
成品尺寸：145mm×210mm
印　　张：4.25
字　　数：41 千字
------------------------------------------------------------
版　　次：2024 年 1 月 第 1 版
印　　次：2024 年 1 月 第 1 次印刷
定　　价：55.00 元
------------------------------------------------------------

扫码获取数字资源

四川大学出版社
微信公众号

本社图书如有印装质量问题，请联系发行部调换

# 成都市实验中学国际理解读本

# 序　言

## 互鉴共赏　西去东归

2021年5月31日，习近平总书记在主持十九届中央政治局第三十次集体学习时指出：要加快构建中国话语和中国叙事体系，用中国理论阐释中国实践，用中国实践升华中国理论，打造融通中外的新概念、新范畴、新表述，更加充分、更加鲜明地展现中国故事及其背后的思想力量和精神力量……要更好推动中华文化走出去，以文载道、以文传声、以文化人。向世界阐释推介更多具有中国特色、体现中国精神、蕴藏中国智慧的优秀文化。要注重把握好基调，既开放自信也谦逊谦和，努力塑造可信、可爱、可敬的中国形象。

随着全球化时代的到来，各国积极推进国际理解教育的理论和实践研究，并在中小学开展国际理解教育。2016年《中国学生发展核心素养》总体框架正式发布，在第五大素养"责任担当"中有对国际理解的明确诠释：具有全球意识和开放的心态，了解人类文明进程和世界发展动态；能尊重世界多元文化的多样性和差异性，积极参与跨文化交流，关注人类面临的全球性挑战，理解人类命运共同体的内涵与价值。2021年版《义务教育英语新课程标准》明确指出：英语课程有利于学生体验中外文化差异，丰富思维方式，增进国际理解，提高人文素养。

《丝路环游记》讲述的是四个中外小朋友在大熊猫华仔的带领下，从成都出发到嵩山少林寺，得到长老指点修行武术后，为完成长老的心愿到了北京的长城，找到修建长城的英雄马汉留下的信件，再护送这份宝贵的文献到陕西省历史博物馆。馆长为了感谢小朋友的贡献，特意邀请他们作为文化小使者进行一场丝路之旅。他们从西安出发到达撒马尔罕、伊斯坦布尔、雅典、罗马、开罗等丝路文化名城。文化小使者们一路学习丝路文化，体会多元文明，他们的事迹引起了联合国教科文组织的关注，最后被邀请到联合国总部做"我们的丝路梦"主旨演讲。

针对学龄段：六年级至九年级（12岁至15岁）。

内容设计：分三部分11个单元，每单元分四个板块。第一板块（Section A）是基础语法单句教学；第二板块（Section B）是与该单元主题相关的对话和连贯的故事情节；第三板块（Section C）是两篇紧扣单元主题的文章，其中A篇是与单元话题相关的有一定深度和趣味性的文章，B篇是与丝路文化相关的深化国际理解的文章；第四板块是练习题，以及词汇、短语。

读本紧扣小初衔接和人教版英语教材，是了解世界多元文化的窗口，是中小学生拓展国际视野、培养国际规则意识的钥匙。最重要的是该读本结合了"一带一路"倡议，有助于学生在故事性和趣味性很强的旅行和探险中体会中华传统文化的魅力、丝绸之路的重要历史意义及丝路沿线文化和习俗的差异。让他们在文化上有传承和发扬，在思想上有继承和创新，充分理解国际化课程的意义，从而树立对中华民族传统文化的自信，建构全球视野，提升国际合作意识，成长为能用双语讲述中国故事且具有中华情怀的人类命运共同体建设者。

李国忠

2023年10月

# 目录

Emily   Mark   Huazai   Lanlan   Xiaolong

"

Huazai, the protagonist, is a giant panda, who is smart, kind, lively and outgoing. Xiaolong and Lanlan are classmates who love traditional Chinese culture, telling Chinese stories and are hospitable. Mark and Emily are young foreign students who came to China to learn Chinese and are also fans of Huazai. And these Chinese and foreign children had a chance encounter with Huazai at the Chengdu Rearch Base of Giant Panda Breeding.

"

Huazai and the other four children met in Chengdu and they enjoyed the local tea culture there. They were invited to send Emei Tea to Shaolin Temple so they set off from Chengdu to Luoyang, where they were instructed by the abbot to practice martial arts. In order to fulfill the abbot's wish, they went to the Great Wall, found the bamboo slips left by Ma Han and started their magical cultural adventure.

# Come and Meet Huazai

Four Chinese and foreign children met at Chengdu Research Base of Giant Panda Breeding, where they were warmly welcomed by Huazai, the giant panda, and made friends with each other.

Xiaolong    Hello! I am Xiaolong. I'm
from Chengdu.
This is my friend Lanlan.
She is from Beijing.
They are my friends,
Mark and Emily. They are
from New York.

**Huazai**　Hello，I am Huazai（华仔）.
Welcome to Chengdu Research
Base of Giant Panda Breeding.
Nice to meet you.

**Kids**　Nice to meet you too.

**Huazai**   Hi, I am Huazai. I am from Chengdu.

**Xiaolong**   Hello, I am Xiaolong. This is my friend Lanlan.

**Lanlan**   Hi, I am from Beijing.

**Mark**   My name is Mark. Emily and I come from New York.

**Emily**   Nice to meet you.

**Huazai**   Nice to meet you too. Welcome to Chengdu.

**Mark and Emily**   Thank you. We love the Giant Pandas.

## Cultural reading A

Hello, I am Huazai. I have big black eyes. I am a little fat, but I am good at climbing. I was born in Chengdu Research Base of Giant Panda Breeding. My favorite food is bamboo. I like sleeping and making friends. Aunt Wang and Uncle Huang look after me like my parents. We love each other.

## Cultural reading B

I am Mark. I'd like to introduce my family. My grandpa likes reading. My grandma likes shopping. My father is an engineer. My mother is a teacher. My uncle likes sports. My aunt likes singing. My sister is 10 years old. I love my family and they love me very much.

I. Match the words in column A and B.

   A                         B

   I live in                 bamboo

   My grandpa likes          engineer

   My father is an           reading

   My favorite food is       shopping

   My grandma likes          Chengdu Research Base of Giant
                             Panda Breeding

II. Act the conversation in Section B out.

III. Read cultural reading A and B and make the right choice.

1. Is Huazai a little fat?

   A. Yes, he is.

   B. No, he isn't.

   C. We don't know.

2. Huazai is good at _____.

   A. reading          B. shopping          C. climbing

3. Aunt Wang and Uncle Huang look after Huazai like _____.

   A. friends          B. parents          C. engineer

grandfather    *n.*   外公；爷爷

grandmother    *n.*   外婆；

   奶奶

engineer    *n.*   工程师

singing    *n.*   歌唱

favorite    *adj.*   最喜欢的

giant panda    *n.*   大熊猫

be good at   擅长

come from   来自

make friends   交朋友

I was born...   我出生于……

My favorite food is...

   我最喜欢的食物是……

# A Phone Call from Tea House

Huazai invited the children to drink tea at a tea house in Kuanzhai Alley where they experienced the life of the locals and learned about Chinese tea culture. Also, they received a mission to deliver tea to the Shaolin Temple.

**Lanlan**   People in China like drinking tea.

**Mark**   I like drinking Cola. Emily likes drinking coffee.

**Huazai**   Wow, I can't drink Cola and coffee. I am afraid they are bad for my teeth.

**Kids**   Then, you can't eat bamboo with bad teeth.

**Huazai**   You are right!

Ding, ding, ding... ( The phone is ringing. )

**Xiaolong**   Hello, who's that speaking?

**Huazai**   Hi, is that Xiaolong? This is Huazai speaking.

**Xiaolong**   Hi, Huazai, this is Xiaolong. How are you?

**Huazai**   Fine. My friend Zhuzhu invites you and your friends to drink tea at her tea house tomorrow afternoon. Are you free then?

**Xiaolong**   Yes and thank Zhuzhu for this invitation. We will be there on time.

**Huazai**   See you tomorrow.

**Xiaolong**   See you.

## Cultural reading A

If you come to Chengdu, don't miss Kuanzhai Alley. It is made up of a broad alley, a narrow alley and across alleys, among which, there are a lot of traditional courtyards, or Siheyuan.

There are many tea houses in Siheyuan. Zhuzhu invites them to drink some green tea. She also introduces black tea, dark tea, white tea, and oolong tea to them. Drinking tea in China is more than the taste of tea. It means a way of life to relax and share all kinds of feelings with friends. Then Zhuzhu shows them a traditional tea ceremony.

At the end of the tea party, Zhuzhu asks Huazai and his friends to send a newly made Emei Tea to Shaolin Temple. There is a mysterious gift waiting for them.

## Cultural reading B

### Ancient Tea-Horse Road

The history of Ancient Tea-Horse Road could date back to the eighth century. This road is located in the southwest of China, with more than 4000 kilometers long. It connected people who exchanged tea for medicine, horses and so on, in provinces such as Sichuan, Yunnan and Xizang.

Half the road was rocky, cliffy and dangerous, and still is even today. The perseverant Chinese people carried bundles of Chinese tea on horses' back over valleys and mountains to Vietnam, to Laos, to Myanmar, and eventually to the coast of the Red Sea in West Africa. In this way, Chinese tea and Chinese tea culture gradually spread to the whole world.

Tea-trading allowed people from different areas to get what they needed, and also maintained the stability of the border. So it is also said that Ancient Tea-Horse Road is a road of business, a road of culture and a road of communication.

People along Ancient Tea-Horse Road did what the world needs today: seeking harmony in diversity, cooperation in spite of all the obstacles and difficulties. On today's time-tested road, China is once again standing out and provides China's solution to global issues.

I. Match the words in column A and B.

| A | B |
|---|---|
| Huazai likes to eat | Siheyuan |
| Drinking too much Cola | a show of making tea |
| See you! | Good bye! |
| traditional courtyards | bamboo |
| a tea ceremony | is bad for teeth |

II. Act the conversation in Section B out.

III. Read cultural reading A and B and make the right choice.

1. Zhuzhu invites them to drink some tea and she introduces black tea, green tea, dark tea, _____ to them.

    A. white tea    B. oolong tea    C. Both A and B

2. Ancient Tea-Horse Road is located in _____.

    A. the northeast of China

    B. the southwest of China

    C. the southeast of China

3. Ancient Tea-Horse road is a road of business, a road of culture and a road of _____.

    A. dinking    B. sightseeing    C. communication

Cola   *n.*   可乐

coffee   *n.*   咖啡

be bad for sth.   对……有害

invite sb. to do sth.

邀请某人去做某事

invitation   *n.*   邀请

Kuanzhai Alley   宽窄巷子

black tea   红茶

the taste of...   ……的味道

relax   *v.*   放松

share   *v.*   分享

traditional   *adj.*   传统的

ceremony   *n.*   仪式

a newly made   新制成的

temple   *n.*   寺庙

mysterious   *adj.*   神秘的

Ancient Tea-Horse Road

茶马古道

be located in   位于某地

cliffy   *adj.*

陡峭的；多悬崖的

perseverant   *adj.*

不屈不挠的；锲而不舍的

bundles   *n.*   束；捆

Vietnam   *n.*   越南

Laos   *n.*   老挝

Myanmar   *n.*   缅甸

eventually   *adv.*   最终

maintain   *n.*   维持

stability   *n.*   稳定

obstacles   *n.*   障碍；阻碍

time-tested   *adj.*

经受时间考验的

global issues   全球问题

# A Gift from Shaolin Temple

Huazai and the children arrived at the Songshan Shaolin Temple in Henan, where they learned the Shaolin spirit of martial arts, morality first, and a little Shaolin Kung Fu from the abbot. And then the abbot gives them a mission to go to the Great Wall to find some lost bamboo slips.

**Lanlan**  Shaolin Temple, here we are!

**Emily**  I like this old temple. It's amazing!

**Mark**  I like Shaolin Kung Fu. It's cool!

**Huazai**   Wow, I like Shaolin Kung Fu too.
It's powerful!

**Kids**   We like *Kung Fu Soccer*. It's fun!

**Huazai**   I like it too. Look at me!

**Fangzhang**   Thank you for your Emei Tea. It smells pleasant and tastes fresh.

**Kids**   Wow! We are glad that you like it.

**Fangzhang**   Do you like Shaolin Kung Fu?

**All the kids**   Yes, of course.

**Fangzhang**   Your friend Zhuzhu asked me to teach you a little Shaolin Kung Fu as a gift.

**Kids**   That's great! Thank you.

**Fangzhang**   Why do you like Shaolin Kung Fu?

**Mark**   Because it's cool and powerful!

**Xiaolong**   It's a way to be strong.

**Emily**   It's a way of keeping healthy!

**Huazai**   I want to be Kung Fu Panda!

**Fangzhang**   You are smart! Shaolin Kung Fu is not to show or beat someone but to keep healthy and help the weak.

**Kids**   Got it!

**Fangzhang**   Ok, let's begin now.

## Cultural reading A

Shaolin Temple is located in Songshan County, Henan Province. It is one of the most famous temples in China. There are many monks practicing Shaolin Kung Fu in the yard. Now Shaolin Kung Fu is becoming more and more popular around the world because it could help people keep healthy and learn Chinese culture.

The children practiced Shaolin Kung Fu very hard. One month later, they all finished the studying. Fangzhang came and gave them a map. He asked them to find some lost bamboo slips at the Great Wall. These bamboo slips are mysterious and with a moving story.

a g i f t f r o m s h a o l i n t e m p
a g i f t f r o m s h a o l i n t e m p
a g i p

## Cultural reading B

Bruce Lee is the English name of Li Xiaolong. He is a super star, martial artist and the founder of Jeet Kune Do. He was born in San Francisco in November 1940 in a famous Chinese opera singer's family. Bruce moved to Hong Kong and soon became a child star in the growing Hong Kong film industry. His first film was called *The Birth of Mankind*. His last film which was uncompleted at the time of his death in 1973 was called *Game of Death*. He acts the leading role in the Kung Fu movies, and Chinese Kung Fu is also world-famous along with it. In many foreign language dictionaries, they all appeared a new word:"Kung Fu". In many foreigners' minds, Kung Fu was the Chinese martial arts. He continues to influence the world deeply as a Kung Fu hero till today.

a g i p
a g i f t f r o m s h a o l i n t e m p
a g i f t f r o m s h a o l i n t e m p

I. Match the words in column A and B.

| A | B |
|---|---|
| The mysterious gift is | fresh |
| Emei Tea tastes | important |
| Mark likes Kung Fu because it is | famous |
| The bamboo slips are | cool and powerful |
| Bruce Lee is very | learning Shaolin Kung Fu |

II. Act the conversation in Section B out.

III. Read cultural reading A and B and make the right choice.

1. Why is Shaolin Temple more and more popular?

   A. People are living healthily.

   B. It's part of Chinese culture.

   C. Both A and B.

2. What made Bruce Lee famous?

   A. He is handsome.

   B. He won many matches.

   C. His Kung Fu in his films.

3. What did Fangzhang ask them to find?

   A. Some lost bamboo slips.          B. A map.

   C. A kind of Kung Fu.

a way of doing/to do...

做某事的方法

amazing   *adj.*

令人惊异的；神奇的

pleasant   *adj.*

令人愉悦的；可爱的

powerful   *adj.*   强大的

strong   *adj.*

坚强的；强壮的

healthy   *adj.*   健康的

monk   *n.*   僧人

popular   *adj.*

流行的；大众的

mysterious   *adj.*   神秘的

moving   *adj.*   感人的

founder   *n.*   创始人

Jeet Kune Do   截拳道

uncompleted   *adj.*

未完成的

the leading role   主角

martial artist   武术家

influence   *v.*   影响

deeply   *adv.*   深深地

till   *conj.*   直到……

# The Lost Bamboo Slips at the Great Wall

The children found the lost ancient slips and learned the touching story of Ma Han, the hero who was one of the workforce to build the Great Wall.

**Lanlan**  The Great Wall is the symbol of China.

**Mark**  The Great Wall must be very long!

**Xiaolong**  Where can we find the lost bamboo slips?

**Emily**   We need to use the map.

**Huazai**   The map must be helpful! I can't
wait to start our wonderful trip!

**Xiaolong**   Huazai, do you know how long the Great Wall is?

**Huazai**   Well, it is 21196.18 kilometers long.

**Xiaolong**   Yes, you are right! There is an old saying in China: He who has never been to the Great Wall is not a true man.

**Mark**   Really? I like to challenge myself. And I also want to find the reason why ancient Chinese built it.

**Emily**   Let's go! The map will lead us to find the lost slips.

Under the guidance of the map, Huazai found a big brick. They moved the brick away and took out a box. There were some old bamboo slips and it was a letter written by a worker more than 2000 years ago!

**All the kids**   We find it!

### Cultural reading A

Huazai opened the letter with a sense of respect. It says...

I am Ma Han (马汉) from Xianyang. This is the third year of Emperor Qinshihuang. I have been working here to build the Great Wall for two years. Many people who came from my village died of illnesses or overwork. I am weak now and I don't know how long I will live. But I will not give up because our Emperor told us building the Great Wall is to protect Qin Empire. The Great Wall can stop the Huns from killing us or our families. I hope the one who finds my letter can bring it back to my hometown. Taking it home is to take my soul home!

## Cultural reading B

The Great Wall winds its way across North China like a massive dragon, crossing mountains, valleys, and deserts before arriving at the sea. As one of the seven wonders of the world, the Great Wall is the longest wall on the Earth, spanning over 6000 kilometers long and rising in an average of 25 feet high.

The Great Wall was built almost 2000 years ago, whose initial section was constructed throughout the Spring and Autumn Period. During the Qin, Ming, and Qing dynasties, all of the walls were connected. Without access to modern machinery, constructing a wall of this kind was extremely challenging in the past. Every task was completed by hand.

In the past, it was used to prevent rivals from invading. Nowadays, people from all over the world have been drawn to the Great Wall. What's more, a large number of people are familiar with the well-known saying in China, "He who does not reach the Great Wall is not a true man."

# Exercise

I. Match the words in column A and B.

| A | B |
|---|---|
| the Great Wall | in the Spring and Autumn period |
| can't wait! | were used before paper |
| massive | was built to protect people |
| bamboo slips | very large, heavy and solid |
| The initial section was constructed | wish to do |

II. Act the conversation in Section B out.

III. Read cultural reading A and B and make the right choice.

1. How long has Ma Han been working to build the Great Wall?

    A. One year.          B. Two years.

    C. Three years.

2. What is true of the Great Wall?

    A. Span less 6000 kilometers long.

    B. Rise in an average 25 feet high.

    C. It was easy to build it.

3. In the past, it was used to prevent _____ from invading.

    A. visitors          B. rivals

    C. foreigners

symbol   *n.*   象征

the Great Wall   长城

helpful   *adj.*   有帮助的

kilometer   *n.*   千米

He who has never been to the
   Great Wall is not a true man.
   不到长城非好汉。

brick   *n.*   砖；砖块

      *adj.*   用砖做的

respect   *n.*   尊敬

      *vt.*   尊重

illness   *n.*   疾病

soul   *n.*   灵魂

massive   *adj.*

   大而重的；大规模的

span over   跨过

average   *n.*   平均

initial   *adj.*   最初的

construct   *v.*   建造；组成

      *n.*   构想

throughout   *prep.*

   贯穿整个时期

access to   接近；进入

machinery   *n.*   机械；机器

extremely   *adv.*   极度；非常

challenge   *n.*   挑战；难题

beneath   *prep.*

   在……之下；低于

      *adv.*   在下面

perish   *v.*   死亡；湮灭

prevent from   阻止

rival   *n.*   对手；敌手

      *v.*   与……相匹敌

      *adj.*   竞争的

invade   *v.*

   武力入侵；侵扰

# Part

In order to fulfill Ma Han's wish, the children escorted the valuable bamboo slips to the Shaanxi History Museum. In recognition of their feat of protecting the precious slips, the curator invited them to retrace the Silk Road as Little Cultural Envoys, bringing the new changes and new stories of China to the Silk Road. Thus, they started their magical journey along the Silk Road.

# Chang'an—The Start of the Silk Road

The children brought Ma Han's bamboo slips to the Shaanxi History Museum, where they were commended by the curator and invited to retrace the Silk Road as Little Cultural Envoys.

**Emily**   Where is Xianyang?

**Xiaolong**   It's in the West of China.

**Lanlan**   Xianyang was the ancient capital city of Qin Dynasty.

**Mark**   Where can we put Ma Han's bamboo slips?

**Huazai**   I think the Shaanxi History
Museum is the right place!

**Kids**   Great! Time to bring our hero
home!

**Huazai** Where is Shaanxi History Museum?

**Xiaolong** I have a map. Let me see... Oh, go down Chang'an Central Road, then turn left at Xiaozhai. Go down Xiaozhai East Road and the museum is on our left.

**Lanlan** It's clear and we won't miss it. Let's go!

**Museum director** Welcome to Shaanxi History Museum. What can I do for you, kids?

**Xiaolong** We came from the Great Wall and brought a letter written by Ma Han over 2000 years ago. Here you are.

**Museum director** Wow, the bamboo slips are so beautiful! They are very important for us to learn the life of Xianyang people and the history of building the Great Wall.

**Huazai** Yes, and the writer named Ma Han asked us to bring his soul home.

**Museum director** This is home for him. We will put the precious bamboo slips into a glass box. Then, people around the world can have a look.

**Huazai**    We are glad to do such a meaningful thing.

**Museum director**    Well, I invite all of you to go on a wonderful Silk Road Trip as Little Cultural Envoys.

## Cultural reading A

The Silk Road which connects Western and Eastern civilizations is the most well-known ancient trade road. It started from Chang'an in Han Dynasty, followed the Great Wall to the northwest and ended at the east shore of the Mediterranean Sea. It links up China and the West. It not only helps Chinese silk, tea, porcelains go to the West but the Western artworks, jewels, spices, and ways of life go into China. At the same time, the peace, prosperity and friendship are shared along the Silk Road with the world.

The four great inventions of China are introduced into Europe through the Silk Road. They are called compass, paper making, gunpowder, and printing.

Besides the trade of goods, the Silk Road spreads Confucianism to Europe and brings China Western arts and cultures. The Silk Road has been buried into the sand for centuries. And now it is time to rebuild and make it shining as all human beings' common treasure.

## Cultural reading B

The Big Wild Goose Pagoda was built in the Daci'en Temple of Chang'an City, Tang Dynasty, also known as the "Ci'en Temple Pagoda".

In the year of 652 AD, Xuanzang designed the Goose Pagoda and led the construction work for the preservation of the Buddhist scriptures and statues brought back to Chang'an from Lndia through the Silk Road.

The Big Wild Goose Pagoda is a seven-story pagoda seen today, with a height of 64.517 meters and a bottom edge length of 25.5 meters. After more than 1370 years of ups and downs, the Big Wild Goose Pagoda stands tall, witnessing Xuanzang's defiance of hardships and dangers to conduct cultural exchanges, and then bring Buddhist scriptures to Chang'an and translate them into Chinese. *The Great Tang Dynasty Records of the Western Regions* written by Xuanzang is the most powerful evidence of the friendly cultural exchanges between China and countries along the Silk Road.

I. Match the words in Column A and B.

A                                    B

ancient                              is stored in Shaanxi
                                     History Museum

the Silk Road                        on our left

the Big Wild Goose Pagoda            a seven-story building

the precious bamboo slips            very old

the museum is                        a trade road between
                                     China and the West

II. Act the Conversation in Section B out.

III. Read cultural reading A and B and make the right
   choice.

1. When did the Silk Road begin?

   A. Qin Dynasty.            B. Han Dynasty.

   C. Tang Dynasty.

2. The Silk Road brings _____ into China.

   A. artworks, jewels

   B. spices, and ways of life

   C. Both A and B.

3. The four great inventions are _____ .

   A. paper, silk, porcelains, hot pot

   B. tea, silk, paper, the Great Wall

   C. compass, paper making, gunpowder, and printing

bring  *v.*  带来

hero  *n.*  英雄

museum  *n.*  博物馆

precious  *adj.*  珍贵的

trade  *n.*  贸易

ancient  *adj.*  古老的

history  *n.*  历史

director  *n.*  主管

around the world  全世界

as  *prep.*  作为

little  *adj.*  年纪小的

cultural  *adj.*  文化的

envoy  *n.*  使节；使者

dynasty  *n.*  王朝

follow  *v.*  沿着

through  *prep.*  通过

artworks  *n.*  艺术品

civilizations  *n.*  文明

shore  *n.*  海岸

the Mediterranean Sea
  地中海

porcelain  *n.*  瓷器

compass  *n.*  指南针

paper making  造纸术

gunpowder  *n.*  火药

printing  *n.*  印刷术

discover  *v.*  发现

besides  *prep.*  除了

spread  *n.*  传播

Confucianism  *n.*  儒家学说

bury  *v.*  埋葬

treasure  *n.*  财宝

the Big Wild Goose Pagoda
  大雁塔

the Daci'en Temple  大慈恩寺

construction  *n.*  建筑；建造

preservation  *n.*  保护；保存

Buddhist scriptures  佛教经书

*The Great Tang Dynasty
  Records of the Western
  Regions*  《大唐西域记》

witness  *v.*  见证；目睹

defiance  *n.*  无视；蔑视

evidence  *n.*  证据；证明

# Samarkand—The Golden Bond on the Silk Road

The Little Cultural Envoys came to the golden bond on the Silk Road—Samarkand. By admiring the wall paintings, they not only learned about Samarkand, but also learned about the remains of the prosperous Tang Dynasty.

**Huazai**   What nice weather it is!

**Lanlan**   Yes, it's sunny and warm.

**Xiaolong**   Fine weather brings us good mood. Do you want to watch the wall paintings in the Ambassadors' Hall?

**Mark**   Great! But where are they?

**Emily**  They're in Samarkand, a famous ancient city on the Silk Road in Central Asia.

**Lanlan**  That must be an amazing city.

**Huazai**  I heard there are many stories about Tang Dynasty on the wall paintings.

**The other kids**  Great! Let's go!

**Emily**  Huazai, do you know how long the history of the wall paintings is?

**Huazai**  It can date back to the time between 656 AD and 676 AD.

**Mark**  What kind of Chinese elements can we find on the wall paintings?

**Lanlan**  A lot. There are images of Emperor Gaozong hunting leopards and Empress Wu rafting in a dragon boat.

**Xiaolong**  You really have a good knowledge about history. And we can get more stories from the wall paintings.

**Emily**  Wow, I'm looking forward to knowing more about Samarkand and the remains of the prosperous Tang Dynasty.

**Huazai**  Hahaha, I'm sure we will find them. Let's get going!

## Cultural reading A

Central Asia has always been a necessary route for the Silk Road. When it comes to the Silk Road, no one can avoid one ancient city—Samarkand, Uzbekistan. The rich and fragrant Tang winds blowing in Samarkand have left Chinese elements all along the Silk Road, and the murals in the Ambassadors' Hall in the seventh century are one example. There are images of Emperor Gaozong hunting leopards and Empress Wu rafting in a dragon boat. These murals perfectly realized the effect of "internationalization" of Chinese stories, so that the scene of the prosperous Tang Dynasty was fixed in Samarkand, recording the prosperity of the Silk Road in those years.

## Cultural reading B

Suyab is listed as a World Heritage Site by UNESCO and is believed by most scholars to be the birthplace of the "Shixian" Li Bai. Suyab was an important town in the Western Regions in the Tang Dynasty. It was an essential route for traders from the East and West, as well as for envoys from various countries. Consisting of a castle, two protected inner cities and a large suburb surrounded by two circular walls, Suyab was a key transfer station on the Silk Road. People gathered here, making Suyab prosperous. The ancient Silk Road, which closely linked Kyrgyzstan and China together, and the birthplace of Li Bai have given new meaning to the traditional ties and friendship between the two countries.

I. Match the words in column A and B.

a good mood        a wall painting

have a good knowledge     a happy feeling
   about

look forward to        an important traffic stop

a mural            know something well

a key transfer station     expect to

II. Share with your partner what you know about the murals from Section A and B.

III. Read cultural reading A and B and make the right choice.

1. The murals in the Ambassadors' Hall are built in _____.

   A. 7th century     B. 17th century     C. 6th century

2. Scholars believed that Suyab is the birthplace of _____.

   A. Li Bai        B. Li Mu        C. Du Fu

3. The building structure of Suyab is not included _____.

   A. a large suburb   B. two circular walls

   C. three inner cities

Samarkand    *n.*    撒马尔罕

Uzbekistan    *n.*
乌兹别克斯坦

Suyab    *n.*    碎叶城

Kyrgyzstan    *n.*
吉尔吉斯斯坦

mood    *n.*    情绪

ambassador    *n.*    大使

Ambassadors' Hall    大使厅

date back to    追溯到

element    *n.*    基本要素

leopard    *n.*    豹

raft    *v.*    漂流

have a good knowledge
about...
对……有很好的了解

look forward to    期待

remains    *n.*    遗迹

prosperous    *adj.*    繁荣的

route    *n.*    路线

avoid    *v.*    避免；回避

fragrant    *adj.*    芳香的

murals    *n.*    壁画

internationalization    *n.*
国际化

record    *v.*    记录

World Heritage Site
世界遗址

UNESCO
联合国教科文组织

birthplace    *n.*    出生地

scholar    *n.*    学者

Western Regions    西域

it's was an essential route for...
这是……的必经之路

various    *adj.*    各种各样的

consist of    由……构成

suburb    *n.*    城郊

surround    *v.*    围绕，环绕

a key transfer station
一个重要的中转站

gather    *v.*    聚集

link... and...
链接……和……

# Istanbul—The Bridge Between China and Europe

The Little Cultural Envoys went to Istanbul, a famous historical and cultural city on the boundary of Asia and Europe, where they learned the story of the Silk Road post "Luotuo Gong" and different customs, cultures and etiquette.

**Lanlan**   Look!
How beautiful it is!

**Emily**   What a beautiful mosque!

**Mark**   Oh! Amazing!

**Huazai**   Wow! How wonderful a city it is!

**Kids**   We like to visit the Blue Mosque!

**Huazai**   Me too! Let's go!

**Huazai**   Hey! Do you smell it?

**Xiaolong**   Yes! How inviting it is!

**Mark**   I think it's the smell of Turkish barbecue. Let's have a look!

**Lanlan**   Wow! I want to have a try. I am so hungry.

**The kids**   Me too!

**Mark**   Is it mutton?

**Huazai**   Yes, but more than that!

**Xiaolong**   Really? What other meat?

**Huazai**   Turkish barbecue or Doner Kebab includes the meat of mutton, beef and chicken.

**Xiaolong**   Why dose it look so nice and taste so great?

**Huazai**   Because the chef added salt, yogurt, milk to the meat, and greased it with oil, then used a thick iron rod to thread the meat piece by piece to make a huge meat ball. The chef kept turning the iron bars for grilling till the color you see.

**Xiaolong**   OK! How knowledgeable you are!

## Cultural reading A

Istanbul is situated at the entrance to the Black Sea. It is Turkey's largest city. Because it is located in both Europe and Asia, Istanbul is the necessary passage for goods coming and going from Asia to Europe. The Seljuk Empire took many measures to keep the trade secure and prosperous. They built some stations every 30—40 kilometers on the Silk Road since the distance is exactly what a caravan can cover in 8—10 hours. The station is called "Camel Palaces" or Kervan Sarayi for the vehicle is camel. The "Camel Palaces" are rectangular in shape, with hard walls and wide gates that make them look like fortresses. The courtyards of the caravans were generally open-air, and there were many rooms and corrals for merchants and their livestock and goods to rest and store. It is also for the merchants to sell and buy their goods. Nowadays, these "Camel Palaces" have been rebuilt into modern hotels. Huazai and the kids tried the Doner Kebab and Turkish Ice Cream so they had a good time and made many new friends there.

### Cultural reading B

The Blue Mosque is one of the most important mosques in Istanbul. It is also one of the famous ten wonders in the world. It is called Blue Mosque because all the walls decorated with blue and white lznik tiles. The huge dome is surrounded by six minarets and the whole construction was completed without a nail. People could visit the Blue Mosque for free and the best seasons to visit it are spring and autumn. Here we can appreciate the unique architecture, calligraphy and carpets, which offers us the experience of the integration and coexistence of diverse cultures.

I. Match the words in column A and B.

| A | B |
|---|---|
| mosque | enjoy oneself |
| inviting | trade groups |
| have a good time | a temple for Muslim |
| trade caravans | like something best |
| favorite | something is pleasing |

II. Act the conversation in Section B out.

III. Read cultural reading A and B and make the right choice.

1. Istanbul is situated _____ the entrance _____ the Black Sea.

   A. on; of          B. at; in        C. at; of

2. It is called Blue Mosque because _____ .

   A. all the walls are in Arabia style

   B. all the walls are blue and white

   C. all the walls decorated with blue and white lznik tiles

3. People could visit the Blue Mosque _____ .

   A. freely          B. for free     C. after buying tickets

Istanbul    *n.*  伊斯坦布尔

Turkish    *n.*  土耳其

Blue Mosque    蓝色清真寺

Doner Kebab    土耳其烤肉

chef    *n.*  厨师

add to    添加

yogurt    *n.*  酸奶

grease    *v.*  为…涂油

rod    *n.*  枝条

thread    *v.*  穿线；穿过

piece by piece    一片一片的

grill    *v.*  烧烤

knowledgeable    *adj.*
    博学的

trade caravan    商旅

one of...    其中之一

what else    别的什么

entrance    *n.*  入口

vehicle    *n.*  交通工具

have a good time    玩得愉快

situate    *v.*  位于

stage    *n.*  驿站

Luotuo Gong
    骆驼宫（即Kervan Sarayi，
    丝绸之路上土耳其驿站名
    称，源于汉语）

fortress    *n.*  堡垒

corral    *n.*  围栏

merchant    *n.*  商人

tile    *n.*  瓷砖；地砖

dome    *n.*  穹顶；圆屋顶

minaret    *n.*  尖塔

without    *prep.*  没有

nail    *n.*  钉子

season    *n.*  季节

for free    免费地

calligraphy    *n.*  书法

integration    *n.*  融合

coexistence    *n.*  共存

diverse    *adj.*  多样的

# European Cultural City—Athens

Athens is an important city on the ancient Silk Road and the birthplace of the ancient Olympic Games. Here, the Little Cultural Envoys learned about the ancient Greek civilization, visited the famous Acropolis site and enjoyed the scenery of the Aegean Sea.

**Lanlan**   Wow! Who is he?

**Emily**   He is Socrates. He is a famous thinker and educator in ancient Greek.

**Mark**   Hey, who is Homer?

**Huazai**   Oh, he is a well-known poet in Athens.

**Xiaolong**   Who is Archimedes?

**Huazai**   I know. He is the father of mechanics
and a great physicist.
Archimedes's saying: Give me a
fulcrum, I can move the Earth!

**Huazai**  Who is Athena?

**Mark**  She is the goddess of wisdom and courage. She is the daughter of Zeus in Greek mythology.

**Xiaolong**  Oh, I know a famous Japanese comic! Saint Seiya.

**Lanlan**  Right, my mother once read it to me.

**Kids**  Haha, that must be interesting!

**Mark**  Athena is very beautiful. She controls laws and orders. She founded the first court in Athens. She is the leader of the Olympus. In ancient Greek, every city adores her so Athens was named after Athena!

**Huazai**  We can be Saint Seiyas to protect Athena and defeat the monsters.

## Cultural reading A

Greece is the first important European country as the Silk Road stretches to the West. Athens is the capital of Greece. It is one of the oldest cities all over the world. Athens is the economic, political and cultural center of Greek. It is a city surrounded by three sides of sea. The building of Acropolis in Athens retained the countless beautiful monuments and fine arts so it is regarded as one of the European cultural symbols. In Athens, people can also see the Apollo Temple at Delphi, Olympic stadium complex (奥林匹克运动场建筑群), Knossos Palace (克诺索斯王宫), Epidaurus open-air theatre (埃皮达夫罗斯露天剧场).

The ancient torch-lighting ceremony spreads the Olympic spirits—peace, friendship, progress to the whole world.

Generally, Athens is always seen as the cradle of western civilization. It has a great influence on the development of European and even the world's civilization.

## Cultural reading B

The Aegean Sea is a famous honeymoon resort. The sunsets here are particularly beautiful. Along the blue Aegean Sea are blue and white houses and gardens of grapes. Wherever you stand, you may find it's a feast for eyes. Any pictures you take will be masterpieces which you can only imagine in your dreams.

Long time ago, there was a beautiful legend. A beautiful kind Harpist who was waiting for her Mr. Right (a young king) to come back played the harp every day and cried against the window till her heart went broken. Finally, her last drop of tear became the Aegean Sea.

In fact, the Aegean Sea is the birthplace of three civilizations. They are Scolady (塞科拉底文明), Minoan (米诺斯文明), and Mycenaean (迈锡尼文明). That's why it is thought of as the source of early European civilization.

I. Match the words in column A and B.

A                      B

thinker      He said he could move the earth.

protect      a comic popular among children

wisdom      to keep something safe

Archimedes  very clever

Saint Seiya  a person thinks deeply about something

II. Act the conversation in Section B out.

III. Read cultural reading A and B and make the right choice.

1. Greece is the _____ important European country as the Silk Road _____ to the West.

   A. first; stretches      B. second; stretch

   C. third; stretches

2. According to the legend, the Aegean Sea was from

   _____ .

   A. a lake             B. a drop of tear

   C. a river of Greece

3. The ancient torch-lighting ceremony spreads the Olympic spirits of _____ .

   A. peace, friendship, progress

   B. peace, love, friendship

   C. love, kindness, progress

Socrates    苏格拉底

educator    *n.*    教育家

Greece    *n.*    希腊

Greek    *adj.*
希腊人的；希腊的

Homer
荷马（古希腊著名诗人，
著有《荷马史诗》）

well-known    *adj.*
出名的；有名气的

poet    *n.*    诗人

Athens    *n.*    雅典

Archimedes
阿基米德（希腊著名的力
学家）

mechanics    *n.*    力学

Physicist    *n.*    物理学家

fulcrum    *n.*
支点；支撑杠杆的点

Athena    雅典娜

wisdom    *n.*    智慧

courage    *n.*    勇敢

Zeus    宙斯

Greek mythology    希腊神话

comic    *n.*    漫画

Saint Seiya    圣斗士星矢

Acropolis    *n.*
（雅典）卫城

retain    *v.*
保留；保持；保存

European    *adj.*
欧洲的；欧洲人的

economic    *adj.*    经济的

surrounded    *adj.*    环绕

torch-lighting ceremony
圣火点燃仪式

cradle    *n.*    摇篮

# The Ruins of Silk Road in Rome

This time the Little Cultural Envoys came to Rome, Italy, a world cultural city, to learn about the bright civilization of ancient Rome and explore the ruins of the Silk Road. Moreover, ancient Rome was the largest consumer capital of tea, silk and porcelain in the west at that time.

**Emily**  I have a beautiful present from my grandmother.

**Mark**  I have never seen such a delicate silk scarf.

**Huazai**  I have seen many silk clothes in China.

**Xiaolong**   In ancient Rome, silk could
only be seen in the Palace.

**Lanlan**   Let's fly to Rome and look for
the signs on the Silk Road!

**Huazai**  I am looking forward to finding the story about silk in Rome.

**Lanlan**  The Silk Road linked Asia and Europe. At the east and west ends were two of the most prosperous countries—Ancient China and Rome.

**Mark**  I didn't know that Rome has such a long history.

**Emily**  At that time, silk was a very precious thing for people in Europe.

**Xiaolong**  How can it go through so many hardships to Rome?

**Huazai**  The answer remains to be discovered.

Cultural reading A

The Silk Road is the earliest and largest goods and culture exchange route in the history of international trade. It opened up a human social equality mutual trade model. In Han Dynasty, China in the east and Rome in the west are the two biggest ancient civilizations. During the 1st and 2nd century AD, for their development needs, the two countries protected the Silk Road and made the trade available between the East and West with their powerful troops. Ancient Rome was the largest silk, tea and porcelains consuming country in the world while China got ancient Rome's gold, painting and building knowledges.

Cultural reading B

As we all know, silk originated in China. As early as the Yellow Emperor, Chinese began to raise silkworms. During the Rome period, one of Rome's social fashions was to wear Chinese silk clothes. One day, Roman consul Caesar suddenly appeared in the Colosseum in Chinese silk robe. The eyes of all the audiences were all caught by the shining color and noble style. Although the performance of the show is very exciting, the audience focused on Caesar, and whispered where he got such a beautiful dress.

Palace nobles wore silk as a symbol of identity. In the 3rd to 4th century AD, silk fabric became the country's only fashionable dress, and it was as valuable as gold. Because of the importance of silk, "silk war" broke out between the Rome and Persia. The war lasted 20 years and ended with no winner. Because of the war, Romans had to develop their own technology of making silk. In the 13th Century, China's silk technology began to mature in Italy and Italy became the center of the European silk industry. Though thousands of years passed, the legend about silk does not fade away in people's mind.

I. Match the words in column A and B.

| A | B |
|---|---|
| silk | gift |
| delicate | fine |
| prosperous | live through or experience |
| present | lively and profitable |
| go through | a kind of material used to make clothes |

II. Act the conversation in Section B out.

III. Read cultural reading A and B and make the right choice.

1. What made the trade available between Rome and Han Dynasty?

   A. Many goods.　　B. Powerful troops.

   C. Both emperors like silk.

2. Because of the war, Romans had to develop _____ .

   A. a way of life without silk

   B. a way to make silk

   C. a way to go to China by sea

3. Though thousands of years passed, the legend about silk does not _____ in people's mind.

   A. disappear　　　B. forget　　　　C. lose color

delicate  *adj.*  精致的

silk scarf  丝绸围巾

sign  *n.*  痕迹

Asia  *n.*  亚洲

Europe  *n.*  欧洲

hardships  *n.*

艰难（hardship复数形式）

discover  *vi.*  发现

*vt.*  发现；发觉

exchange  *n.*  交换；交流

trade  *n.*  贸易

*vt.*  用……进行交换

porcelain  *n.*  瓷器

Emperor  *n.*  皇帝；君主

audience  *n.*  观众；听众

whisper  *vi.*  耳语

*vt.*  低声说出

technology  *n.*  技术；工艺

fashionable  *adj.*  时尚的

Persia  *n.*  波斯

mature  *adj.*  成熟的

profitable  *adj.*  有利润的

fade away  消退

# An Unforgettable Day in Egypt

The Little Cultural Envoys came to Egypt, and met the symbol of ancient Egypt—Pyramids.

**Xiaolong**  That must be the relics of Alexandria Lighthouse.

**Emily**  Sure, it is one of the world's seven wonders!

**Mark**  Once it was very tall, about 135 meters.

**Lanlan**  It must have been such a magnificent lighthouse standing there.

**Huazai**  With the light of it, ships wouldn't get lost in the dark.

The Little Cultural Envoys ride camels and come to Pyramids of Giza, appreciating the spectacular view of Egypt. Not far from them, an Egyptian girl is introducing the local culture to a group of tourists.

**Huazai**   Guys, have you noticed the guide over there?

**Xiaolong**   Of course! We are so lucky.

**Emily**   So cool. It seems that she knows everything!

**Huazai**   I'm thinking about inviting her...

（The guide is approaching while the Envoys are talking. ）

**The guide**   Excuse me, I'm sorry to interrupt you. You look confused. Is there anything I can do for you?

**Lanlan**   Nice to see you! We are Little Cultural Envoys from China.

**The guide**   China! Really? I've been to China for several times to learn Mandarin and brilliant Chinese culture.

**Huazai**   What a coincidence! We're here to learn Egyptian culture and also look for the stories about the Ancient Silk Road.

**The guide**   What you are doing is so meaningful! Ancient China and ancient Egypt, as two of the Four Ancient Civilizations, share similarities and differences. With your efforts, both countries can improve understanding and friendship.

**Emily**   And the friendship starts from the Silk Road trade.

**The guide**   Exactly! The Silk Road not only allows people from China and Egypt to trade, but also serves as a way for cultural exchanges.

**Lanlan**   You really know a lot! Would you like to come with us and introduce more?

**Xiaolong**   Yeah, we can learn from each other and enjoy each other!

**The guide**   My pleasure.

## Cultural reading A

Who Built Giza Pyramids?

For centuries, the pyramids of Giza have been timeless symbols of Egyptian culture. But who actually built them? For years, we did not know for sure. But archeologists recently discovered an ancient village near the pyramids. Close by, there was also a cemetery where pyramid builders were buried. By studying these places, archeologists can now confirm that the pyramids were not built by slaves or foreigners. Ordinary Egyptians built them.

It took about eighty years to build the pyramids. According to archeologists, about 20000 to 30000 people were involved in completing the task. The workers had different roles. Some dug up the rock, some carried it, and some shaped it into blocks. People also worked on different teams, each group with its own name. On a wall in Khufu's Great Pyramid, for example, a group of workers wrote "Friends of Khufu". The competition between teams often made the work faster.

Life for these workers was hard. The bones show signs of arthritis which developed from carrying heavy things for a long time. Archeologists have also found many female skeletons in the village and cemetery. The damage to their bones is similar to the men's. Their lives may have been even tougher: male workers lived to age 40–45, but women to only 30–35. However, workers usually had enough food, and they also had medical care if they got sick or hurt.

Time, wind and sand took many glories away, but what can be kept in the history is Egyptians' bravery, creativity, hardworking and sacrifice.

## Cultural reading B

### The Egyptian Sphinx

A great symbol of ancient Egypt is the Sphinx, a magnificent monument carved out of a big rock.It sits outstandingly in front of the Pyramids of Giza. It is a carving of the body of a lion with a head of a king, symbolizing strength and wisdom. It is 200 feet long and 65 feet high with paws being 50 feet long. The body of the Sphinx was buried in the sand for thousands of years and only in 1905, about a century ago, the sands was cleared away from it. The Sphinx faces to the east, to the horizon and this has an astronomical belief to the ancient Egyptians. It is thought that it is a guardian of the horizon for the later journey of the kings in the life-after. However, the Sphinx misses some pieces, his ritual beard that is now placed in the British museum while his nose was destroyed by Napoleon's troops who used it as a target in 1798. The Sphinx has undergone many major restorations. The value of Sphinx is widely accepted by people around the world. It is now well kept by Egyptians. So we strongly believe Sphinx is part of human beings' history and will see the rise and fall of us and tell our story in its own way in silence.

I. Match the words in column A and B.

| A | B |
|---|---|
| a lighthouse | a very formal meeting |
| get lost | shows the way on the sea |
| be friendly to | It is believed that |
| an appointment | lose one's way |
| people strongly believe | be good to people |

II. Act the Conversation in Section B out.

III. Read Cultural reading A and B and make the right choice.

1. Alexandria Lighthouse is easy to see because _____.

   A. it's wide    B. it's tall    C. it's long

2. Which one has the Egyptian guide done in China?

   A. Learn Mandarin.            B. Learn travelling.

   C. Learn cooking.

3. Why did Pharaohs in ancient Egypt build Pyramids?

   A. The Pyramids can attract many visitors.

   B. It is one of the seven world wonders.

   C. They believed they have the life-after.

Alexandria Lighthouse
亚历山大港灯塔

Pyramids of Giza
吉萨金字塔群［吉萨金字塔群位于开罗近郊，主要由大金字塔也称胡夫金字塔（Khufu）、哈夫拉金字塔（Khafra）、孟卡拉金字塔（Menkaura）及狮身人面像（Great Sphinx）组成］

Sphinx
斯芬克斯（吉萨的这尊斯芬克斯应是世界上最大最著名的一座，而且是由一整块巨型岩石雕制而成。斯芬克斯身长约73米，高21米，脸宽5米。据说这尊斯芬克斯狮身人面像的头像是按照法老哈夫拉的样子雕成的，作为看护他的永住地——哈夫拉金字塔的守护神）

lighthouse  *n.*  灯塔

Egypt  *n.*  埃及

Egyptian  *n.*  埃及人

one of the seven wonders
七大奇迹之一

magnificent  *adj.*  壮丽的

get lost  迷路了

Pharaoh  *n.*  法老

approach  *v.*  靠近；接近

Mandarin  *n.*  普通话

meaningful  *adj.*  有意义的

archeologist  *n.*  考古学家

close by  在附近

confirm  *v.*  确认

slave  *n.*  奴隶

be involved in  参与；卷入

complete  *v.*  完成

shape... into  做成……形状

competition  *n.*  竞争

skeleton  *n.*  遗骸

arthritis  *n.*  关节炎

tough  *adj.*  艰苦的

live to the age of  活到……岁

sacrifice    *n.*    牺牲

medical care    医疗

challenging    *adj.*    挑战性的

creativity    *n.*    创造

outstandingly    醒目地

symbolize    *v.*    象征; 标志

strength    *n.*    力量

wisdom    *n.*    智慧

paw    *n.*    爪

astronomical    *n.*    天文的

belief    *n.*    信念; 信仰

It is thought that...

　　据认为……

guardian    *n.*    守卫

horizon    *n.*    地平线

the life-after    来世

ritual beard    仪式之须

undergo    *v.*    经历

restoration    *n.*    复原

widely    adv.    广泛地

be well kept    精心保管

the rise and fall    起起落落

The Little Cultural Envoys told Chinese stories along the Silk Road, spread Chinese civilization, learned about the Silk Road culture, respected differences and cherished peace, which triggered the resonance of the people of the countries along the Silk Road. What's more, their efforts also attracted the UNESCO, which invited them to the United Nations Headquarters.

# A Great Speech at the UN Headquarters

The Little Cultural Envoys came to the UN Headquarters, visited the famous cultural sculptures, and learned about the contribution of the UN in maintaining peace, developing economy, popularizing education and eliminating poverty, etc. And Huazai was invited to deliver a speech on "Our Silk Road Dream".

**Emily**   Welcome to New York!

**Xiaolong**   We finally come to the destination of this journey—the UN Headquarters!

**Lanlan**   I've been dreaming to visit "The Knotted Gun". Now it's in my sight!

**Mark**   Here you can see the Security Council, the Building of the United Nations Headquarters and so on.

**Huazai**   If I had a chance to make a speech at the UN, I would invite more children to join us and build a much happier and healthier world!

**Emily**   If I had a chance to work here, I would help the children living in poverty and provide them with enough food and good education!

**Xiaolong**   If I were the Secretary General of the UN, I would stop the wars and lead people of the globe to live a much more peaceful and prosperous life!

**Emily** As we all know, China is now a very important member of the UN. Some people commented that the restoration of New China's lawful seat in the UN attributes to giant efforts from itself and many other countries, and it is also a great event in UN's history. Is that true?

**Xiaolong** Yeah, that is true. It was definitely remarkable, which means that China could speak out for the people from developing countries.

**Mark** So when did New China restore its lawful seat in the UN?

**Huazai** On December 25th 1971, the UN voted to restore the lawful seat of the People's Republic of China.

**Xiaolong** This marks that a quarter of the world's population rejoining the family of nations, which is of great and far-reaching significance to both China and the world.

## Cultural reading A

The Little Cultural Envoys are dressed in nice suits standing in front of the conference hall of the UN Headquarters and Huazai is offered to make a speech.

Dear Secretary General of the UN and friends around the world, good afternoon!

I am Huazai. As you can see, I am from China as a member of the Little Cultural Envoys. One month ago, we had an honor to visit cities on the Silk Road. Along the way, the rise and fall came into our eyes. The rich, various and happy lives of the people came into our mind. The desire for peace, prosperity and understanding came into our heart! We traveled half of the Earth but we didn't feel lonely. Because people along the Silk Road, offered us help and shared a belief with us. This belief is that we humans are equal to enjoy a flourishing and peaceful life! We are brothers and sisters on the way to achieve this dream! We are born to build our Earth home! This Silk Road unites us and allows us to stand hand in hand, heart to heart, to shape a beautiful tomorrow for all of us!

Thank you for your listening!

## Cultural reading B

The United Nations is an intergovernmental international organization composed of sovereign states which was established after World War II. The purposes of the United Nations are to maintain international peace and security, to develop friendly relationships among nations, to promote cooperation in the fields of economy, education, public health, etc. , and to work as the center to coordinate the international affairs of its member countries.

Over the past 52 years, China has contributed a lot to the United Nations. As one of the Five Permanent Members of the Security Council, in recent 30 years, China has participated in nearly 30 UN peacekeeping operations, sending more than 50000 soldiers to over 20 countries and regions, such as Cambodia, Sudan, Lebanon, etc. China has fulfilled its peacekeeping missions, contributing to the settlement of disputes and maintaining regional security and stability of the developing countries. As the largest developing country, China actively supports the United Nations Sustainable Development Agenda and achieves the poverty reduction targets set by the 2030 Agenda for Sustainable Development 10 years ahead of schedule, and the poverty reduction population accounts for more than 70% of the world's poverty population.

China's participating in the UN presents China's image as a responsible country whose mission is to build a community with a shared future for mankind.

I. Choose the right one to complete the sentences.

1. Huazai and his friends had an honor _____.

2. If I were General Secretary of United Nations, _____.

3. The United Nations is _____.

4. As the largest developing country, _____.

5. The UN Headquartes is _____.

A. I would stop the wars.

B. China actively supports the United Nations Sustainable Development Agenda.

C. to walk on the Silk Road

D. an intergovernmental international organization

E. the political center of the United Nations

II. Act the conversation in Section B out.

III. Read cultural reading A and B and make the right choice.

1. Do they travel half of the Earth but they don't feel lonely?

A. Yes, they do. B. No, they didn't. C. Yes, they did.

2. When was the United Nations established?

A. Before World War II.   B. After World War II.

C. After World War I.

3. China is a /an _____ country.

A. developed    B. developing    C. underdeveloped

the United Nations　联合国

headquarters　*n.*　总部

capital　*n.*　首都；省会；资金

political　*adj.*
政治的；党派的

Security Council
（联合国）安理会

restore　*v.*　恢复

far-reaching　*adj.*　深远的

comment　*v./n.*　评论

attribute to　归因于

remarkable　*adj.*　显著的

giant effort　不懈的努力

cultural envoy　文化使者

lawful　*adj.*　合法的

intergovernmental　*adj.*
政府间的

sovereign states　主权国

contribute　*v.*　贡献

sustainable development
可持续性发展

promote　*v.*　促进

cooperation　*n.*　合作

field　*n.*　领域

coordinate　*v.*　协调；配合

international affairs　国际事务

member countries　成员国

poverty　*n.*　贫困

population　*n.*　人口

account for　占据

permanent member
常任理事国

dispute　*n.*　争论；纠纷

developing country
发展中国家

purpose　*n.*　目的

participate　*v.*　参加

mission　*n.*　使命

community　*n.*　共同体

mankind　*n.*　人类

peace　*n.*　和平

maintain　*v.*　维持